FOR THE LOVE OF ENDINGS

Please direct all inquiries to:
Editorial Office
Four Way Books
POB 535, Village Station
New York, NY 10014
www.fourwaybooks.com

Library of Congress Cataloging-in-Publication Data

Names: Purkert, Ben, author.
Title: For the love of endings / Ben Purkert.
Description: New York, NY : Four Way Books, [2018]
Identifiers: LCCN 2017029359 | ISBN 9781945588051 (softcover : acid-free paper)
Classification: LCC PS3616.U783 A6 2018 | DDC 811/.6--dc23
LC record available at https://lccn.loc.gov/2017029359

This book is manufactured in the United States of America and printed on acid-free paper.

Four Way Books is a not-for-profit literary press. We are grateful for the assistance
we receive from individual donors, public arts agencies, and private foundations.

This publication is made possible with funds from the Jerome Foundation.

PROUD MEMBER

[clmp]

We are a proud member of the Community of Literary Magazines and Presses.

Distributed by University Press of New England
One Court Street, Lebanon, NH 03766

FOR THE LOVE OF ENDINGS

Ben Purkert

Four Way Books

Tribeca

for you with me like so

Contents

In life, the number of beginnings is exactly equal to the number of endings.

—Mary Ruefle

TODAY IS WORK

I'm searching for the right verb
for a dead frog. I want one
large but not so full it floods
my eyes. The verb should stand
on its own without support
from viewers like you & you
really are a viewer, it's just
I'm concealed by a series of
tall buildings & significant life
events. If I reach you, call it
lifting a finger & driving
into your skull. I like surgery
to be light. I like a cradle
overflowing with baby gifts &
stuffed-animal aliens, lime-green
to the touch. I'm really happy
for you, for your off-screen
special effects. I want you
exploding like a bridge.

SELF-PORTRAIT AS INFINITE SMALLNESS

every inch of me is
microbes but I'm growing okay
with this, they remind me

who's the boss, who's
the sum of whose
parts & on my block earlier

there was a sudden side
impact, a two-door
smashed open & one

witness kept recounting
who ran the light,
using her two hands

for each wrecking
the other, clapping them
so the sound tore through

the streets & the city's
still a grid, everyone agrees
on this, even the ocean

now is nodding never
once being asked

IF I SHUT MY EYES, WHAT OTHER DOORS IN ME FLY OPEN

I'd like to meet my bones.
I'd strew them on a Minnie Mouse

beach blanket near the water—
her red dress, eyelashes peeking through

my rib cage. Isn't this love: to marry
a plush background? I'd unthread

Minnie's face, stitch it into places
I've lived: each hole in the wall,

each rough winter I've held
against my lips. I remember snow

like it was yesterday, sticking
into the night. But memory is lost

on bones. Flesh, on the other hand,
grasps what it can, while it can:

like the sea takes the shore,
dragging it by the ear.

THE PAST IS THE PRESENT ONLY COLDER

At night, everything feels. Even a river
feels its way through the woods, mumbling.

Slight edge in its voice. Enough to pry
the sky open a crack, then light through

the haze. The earth covers its face
with brush. Flagstones elbow each other

inside a mile-long fence. I can divide
the world into two types of people:

one blankets my streets; the other paves
them right over. I once saw a comedy

where the tuba in a marching band
trips & his fellow instruments

go on trampling him. With each step,
the little in his lungs puffs out

a note. The joke is, nothing changes.
The refrain hits the same peak.

You & I could trade places
& still the water around our lives

would be level. Someday I'll lock
myself away, then flatten my breath

against the glass. I'll leave a smiley
in the fog. All movies end in tragedy,

names leaping off the screen.

NATURAL INTELLIGENCE

The plural of anything is bound to be sharper:

countless birds spelling *V* above my head.

Where they land, the earth must slightly compress,

hardening under their cool weight.

Wing-shadows held against their breasts.

Each bird only tries to be

what it is, & people call this intelligence.

We write it down, star it somewhere in our notes.

When our minds wander, they go alone.

THE LAKE IS A MIND WITH A SHOPPING CART IN IT

See that? A heart on the flap of
your Cheerios box? A bee with white
teeth? Don't faint, or you'll cause
a sharp rise in blackouts around here.
At the register, please hold a ham
upside down if you want it
to scan. Comb the parking lot, blinking
keys, all the flashes the keys were
programmed for. For an escape,
pull over. There really is a lake though
you hear it's frozen & you'll do
donuts on it, while your car strains
to avoid the very obvious
desire to strain. Finally home
you start changing & conceal yourself
with shades. You can nuke yourself
garlic knots. An old white ash
anchors your front lawn, soaks up
a brake light through its leaves.

THE PAST SUFFERS TOO

The bumper sticker says *Live In The Moment!* on a Jeep
that cuts me off. I'm working to forget it, to let go

of everything but the wheel in my hands,
as a road connects two cities without forcing them

to touch. When I drive by something, does it sway
toward me or away? Does it slip into the past

or dance nervously in place? The past suffers
from anxiety too. It goes underground, emerging

once in a blue moon to hiss. I hear the grass never
saying a word. I hear it spreading its arms across

each grave & barely catch a name. My dying wish
is scattering now before every planet. I want places to

look forward to. Listen: the earth is a thin voice
in a headset. It's whispering *breathe . . . breathe . . .*

but who believes in going back?

TIMES THE WHOLE WORLD BY ZERO

Two mirrors stare into each other
& start a family. Anyone else

game to settle down? You know me:
I'll balloon when parked on a sofa.

I'll stuff my face, then string it
above the mantle: another X-mas

light fizzling, blinking out the day.
But I have ideas to get across!

I have a message to deliver
from the future while bursting

into flame. Will my skylight beg
to melt down? Will my TV

crawl on all fours, the remote in
its mouth? How long until that pair

grows distant again? The sun
remains the last place I can go

for warmth. I'll work a little
bomb into this page.

NEARLY A BILLION WINGS

Each Super Bowl, the US consumes nearly
a billion alone: each wing like half of a couple

ignoring the other. Picture them
in a living room, their flat-screen TV

screwed into the wall which assumes a light
strain. Their wings, atomic: spicy as hell.

Let's assume that a bird without wings
has a span of ten seconds left. Then the game

unravels, another Hail Mary fluttering out
of bounds. Fiery, a fan might snap:

Hit the open man in his goddamn hands—

DISASSOCIATED SELF-PORTRAIT FROM
TEN THOUSAND FEET

I could scatter like a lot
full of school buses
picking up small
kids & from up here
roads cut everything
into squares, each
perfect serving
of field, soybeans
corn maybe cotton
& when exactly
will it bloom?
will it take heart in
blooming? the shadow
from my plane falls
then gets dragged over
roofs, the shadow
slicing through a big-
box store Target I think
tomorrow I'll crawl
my way back, pick up
some sheets I'd love
my thread count
in the billions

FOR THE LOVE OF ENDINGS

The blank page always wins. Not because of its blank stare but because it speaks! It makes sense: letters, commas left out in the cold. It skips happily over the mind, heads right for the throat. Let me start there.

I enjoy weeping in convenience stores. At least I'm being recorded on black-&-white film. I'll loop over myself for hours. I'll shoplift simply to nail down my dominant hand. Junk food on the shelf sometimes cries out to me. El Diablo Doritos are screaming my name.

I passed a billboard today that got under my skin. It hurt to drive my car, seeing ads for sleeker cars. What am I, a bad husband? A future pair of wandering eyes? In my dreams, the whole world falls for each other.

I hope the afterlife is one giant pretzel with milk. I'm not talking about *forever*. I'm killing time with snow angels as I sprinkle salt on my drive. Sad little ghosts. If God exists, God exists to disappear.

Spoiler alert: here's my ending. I'm confined to a bed while my mind drifts in & out, like another overworked nurse on her phone. *Nurse!* I shout, but she's already gone. Someone fills in, someone with her same face. *Please*, I say, *give me the truth.* She keeps dancing around it.

Should I bury my face in this book? I have a tired obsession with death—not *real* death, just the moment when my lover loses steam, crashing beautifully on the couch. Her eyes are closed, so I close mine, to be closer to her.

If a cartoon coyote blows up the bridge on which he stands, his dreams go up in smoke. All animated characters are basically homeless, in search of a body. They run around in circles in two dimensions. They fall off cliffs because that's all they have.

The TV reminds me of sunlight. It's nice being burned in the comfort of my own skin. I'll whiten my teeth until they soar through the sky, until they sink themselves suddenly into the moon. Why else go outside? The rain's stuck again in the rain.

In any standing ovation, the cheering fans rise to their feet because, sadly, they block their own view. I can learn from this as a writer: whatever looks like praise is an obstruction of something else.

People are drowning in breaking news. The whole world is watching the world just watching. Even planets are falling in stature, their hearts too slack. Tell me: what song could lift them? How would it go?

I'll name my child *Gloom* because I'd like her to be happy. I want Gloom running free in tall grass, the sun licking the blades at her waist. I want the other children to jump rope with Gloom, maybe braid Gloom's hair. When I was little, I knew a Faith. She never went far.

I like my poems to look me in the eye. They should know their father, know where to stick the knife. When I'm gone, the thing I'll miss is missing, is describing the world I miss. So much depends upon *you*, reader. Look how these words lean on you, not even knowing your name.

DEAR EX

I'm hardly alone—
like most men, I'll gaze

at anything to avoid looking
inward. Like how a stream

reflects what surrounds
but never the face of

itself. I mean *force*, I mean—
forget it. Let's cast ourselves

into a pond: a still surface
standing forever without

a break. Let's freeze at
the tipping point when you

leave me, here in the heart
of this song. At least

metaphors have my back;
at least the swallows outside

my window sound into
each other. I hope they fly

so far south, they don't
remember a thing.

LIKE AN ANIMAL CUT ROUGHLY IN HALF

When person A splits from B, silence walks into the room.

Clock hands inch toward, then away from the sky.
Tables drag their claw feet on the carpet.

Even the mind holds weight, a center of gravity:
somewhere to reach for, to dig & dig deeper.

Until mounds of red earth spring up.
Until the hole takes on groundwater, echoing a well.

Soon a fresh city emerges, a system of pipes, a boatload
of sex shops, people starting over.

They swipe onto trains. They flood parks with kids.
They strip down a kitchen, put in an island.

PASSING THOUGHTS IN A COUPLE

Beauty, books say, is symmetry.

Is pressing two of the same

to kiss. Like holding a stone out

over water, then dipping it

in itself. I draw my fingers out

from you & inch them toward

your mouth. In my head I say

Go on, & this could refer to time

or space. So I pick. I give

myself one. I picture a door

with my hand walking through.

Then all my limbs finally

on the opposite coast.

ONLINE MATCH

Hello, you're now being viewed. Q: *How many floors does your body have?* A: *I fall hard for the perimeter of a girl.* Drag your mouse over the picture to show depth. Deflect the age question with a swift turn. Bury the ex in run-on sentences. Say you'd like more little ones than you'd like. Then sprinkle white lies over coffee. Lock arms around an iceberg wedge with light dressing. If you grow apart, be the bigger person by an inch.

IN HOTELS, SEX FLINGS ITSELF OPEN

the king bed pours out
its frame to the dark

its pillows like a surprise
rock jetty & this time

let's leave the TV on
to watch us   *yes*

let's feel its eyes
burning up your back

first then mine &
we're a knot pulled in

all directions so nothing
can escape not even

our minds reaching
up & up for the ceiling

where hot air lightly
presses its face

RUNNING INTO THE EX

I wasn't expecting you says a tree to the cloud

I tapped your phone says the cloud

Take a hike says the tree

(Mountains & a moth weigh thoughts of each other)

(The sky runs all the way around earth)

Give back my dog says the cloud

Go chew his toys says the tree

(TV pressures the world into diamonds)

(Out of nowhere, the sky spits out a breeze)

Let's fly says the tree

Into what says the cloud

THE WORDS I FAILED TO BE

I'll rip off this Coke label to reveal my love life: the ones I like

enough, the ones I adore but can't ever close. I'm drawn

again to the frozen-food aisle: is this where I meet my new self,

shuddering inside a box of waffles? Hey, a closeout on ice cream,

maybe I'll pile up on rocky road? I won't mince anything:

not the breakup, not hours before, each minute snapping shut

on my wrist. I won't dwell on what I said, only the words

I failed to be. A watermelon, a half-off watermelon, it's over:

because I love the seeds, I spit them out.

TATTOO OF A BUTTERFLY ON A BUTTERFLY

the TV's so loud I start
squinting   I start at
the corner of each eye
bringing it shut just
barely enough to ruffle
a bed sheet   the TV cries
What's Coming Up Next!
but this is far from
the future   each day
the tough skin on a fruit
I always chew I always
leave some light
marks on it   once
on a date a butterfly
lifted her wings to me
she was revealing
some pattern

MIRROR I DON'T KNOW

I'm far from the dead center of things.
No forever talk, just ladyfingers on milk glass.

Each afternoon spent in four coordinates:
Me, Me, Sunlight, Ache. You, leaving warm prints

on whose mirror I don't know. But look,
my scrapped VW still parked on Google Earth!

My street frozen in spring. My roof, its slanted dish.
Somewhere in here too, my sunny death,

a waiting rectangle. Though it's hard to pick out
between pear blossoms & telephone wire.

Dearest pin on my screen, I'll drag & drop you.
I'll hold down on + until I'm larger than life.

To exit this window, I claw my way out.

SETTING BEAR TRAPS FOR MYSELF

A wound is
merely a matter
of time; a woman
is where two roads
merge before
my eyes. Heading
home, a salmon
swims so violently
it leaps out from
its skin. I crave
love like this.
I want nights
that bite my
palms. I'll run
them under ice
water, then bind
with gauze. I can't
help climbing
in age. I throw
myself at any
pretty face.

SALIVATING OVER NOTHING

the mind is so easily
had, it's easily

the first picked-
off deer

from a herd, the one
they all guessed

would go first
but never

said anything & they
let the mind be

ravaged, this way
they might

stand a chance
& it was so

freeing to look on
with no mind!

the thing
swallowed in

seconds, already
a far-away

thought but when
the herd left to

roam they fell
frozen, their

mouths oh-so-
close in the grass

RUNNING INTO THE EX AGAIN

sword toothpicks in Swiss

cubes & the holes are

what we don't say

to each other but still

swallow while shaking

hands in fact we

hardly shake the glass

in our off hands we won't

spill the red no way

aren't we simply

having a ball aren't we

surrounded by our

dearest walls

our hearts always

buried in one chest

or another

MORE MORE

I sometimes want more   than I've got hands for
& what are hands but handles   tied up with

a point-&-shoot or smartphone with a no-
shatter lens   I'd lose my weekend just skimming

this puddle for shadows   now I settle on
a frame   a cattail sticking its neck through the tracks

says something about life   says no trains
say hi anymore   & if this bridge won't give

it'll break off into tangents   see the people across
talk funny   they lose more nouns

to the river each year & what can a city sorry
what *kind* of city   releases its people

to the air without kite strings & sorry what
kind of air   is it hard fluttering under the bit

of a push drill?   a chorus line of clouds I can't see

to the end of?   because my eyes are watery

nearly all water in fact   if I look down

the little I own might pour out

ESCAPE PLANS

One day, night dawns on you.
The stars shooting at you or away,
black holes eating everything

in sight. You see existence
for what it is. You see the gap
between the world & how

people paint it: dark, distant, there
for the taking. So *take*. Moonlight
hitting water, water hitting back.

You leave for a second

to check on something. You return as something else.

Your heart: the silt of a stream.

Your mind: waves breaking on rocks.

Now you're eight whisper-thin legs, scurrying over this page.

Nothing to eat here, you say. What are you hungry for,

other planets?

Look up from these words & they're gone.

When dividing, please show all your work.
Slice everything into all its parts, its up
quarks, down quarks: slivers of mass
hanging on every phrase. Here,

have a gold star. Set it on your tongue.
Now drive off west: let exhaust melt
into the background; let talk radio spin
some dials in your head. As you pass

an arcade, think of Whac-A-Mole:
that point in the game when the mole
pops up faster, everywhere, mallet
striking the holes. Listen: your bones

outnumber your heart. Hear them
huddle around her like wolves.

& you should exit whatever dark place you're in:

leave your date wanting more, then pour out

on the sidewalk. In full sun, who knows how

your cheekbones may photograph. How foreign

your heart may appear. You have a nice body

on your hands. You have your looks good

enough to eat. You can run marathons

with a gun going off in your sleep,

but when you reach your time of death,

be ready for seconds: the doctor will lift you

from a drawer & ask which self to unfreeze.

You can play the field or gravel road

but nothing between.

Everyone you love,

                        leave. It's the law,

like not passing

                        on the right. You can hug

each & every curve

                        you meet, but the rain

is a reason

                        to see yourself

with someone else.

                        If you top the mountain,

what's the point?

                        If you drive to

the lookout, *I'm sorry*

                        what was your name?

HUMILITY

Because I'm washed up, a fraction
of myself. So miniscule I'm sure

someone threw me a garden
party & snipped off the heads of

my guests—those droopy perennial
show-offs. The world's so tired,

it melts down at the core. God,
build me another earth

& this time, really mean it: make me
a snow globe where little townspeople

freeze to death, then are reborn as
flakes shimmering down

from the top. A kind of routine
weather, but in the end, night always

wins: shadow one, object zero.
What a smackdown. A total

slaughter, like an action movie
blowing up everything but the star.

In the background, the extras
bleed into each other.

BLAME GAME

Pin the ozone layer on me:
I drove my Hummer into the sky
when I gunned through a red light.
I hit outer space; I clearly went too far.

It's hard to tweeze apart a hole
from the everyday emptiness of air.
Hard to touch upon a hole & not sail
right through. One day or another

every iceberg flames out. What's left
but punching my own face squarely in
the gap between my teeth? Nothing
hurts like a gap, nothing at all.

DARK PLANETS WE COULD REALISTICALLY FLEE TO

the TV falls the world inside

falls with it   the sun shatters

on the floor the stars all

break open   I'll pause here

for a brief memory: see there

was a honeybee I once as a little

nothing collided with

& all summer he worked

hand in glove with the darkness

from an empty Coke can   I'd hear

fizzling of wings   I figured of all

the rough places to call home

then the comb   ballooned

like a city on the coast

stretching across the decades

until the world was a huge wheel

so many spokes all around

they forked my eye

with light

DRIVING A U-HAUL IN THE DREAM OF ARROWS

a little pink lemonade in the nick of
my thumb, a little radio

static ringing in my lungs & each lung
like a cut-out since the body

can't be everywhere, can't be all things
to all mirrors & if the engine groans

I'll pretend this isn't a U-Haul
but a huge-ass space bot bearing me

in its gaping mouth & the two of us
could toss around ideas for

miles, we could blow by a million
signs lit up, high in the sky with arrows

pointing down & I think maybe
that's what sky is, just a whole mess

of sharp ends & the U-Haul
has something he needs

to say, he nearly breaks down
from not saying it

TOO MUCH

true the dead don't do
squat all day they make real
shitty spokespeople they never
land any parts in TV spots
not even a fly-by-night water
proofer no they can't bring
themselves to smile it would
take too much out of them
they're spent all the time
but still agree to go out
they collide endlessly
in hush-hush underground
night clubs they go *excuse me*
with their hip bones
their conversations are
slightly devoid of substance
what's lacking in the dead
is made up for in being
walked on yes they're all
our relatives so clearly
wrapped up in us

IDEAL WORLD

in an ideal world there's no history:
no chicken before the egg broke
in the beginning there was
light without words for light,
no birds written before wings
the clouds falling apart
without falling, the sea brings
itself to the table & swallows
one sword, the body says what
the body wants, in a world where
plastic bottles are swimming out
to sea & meet & hold hands
singing along, please remember
to hold what you love, the waves
are high, they crash hello
are you there

NO SMALL THING

Not the heart of a plane
but its black box. Not words
but wings scrawled across
a page, almost onto
the next. Am I reading
too much into night?
A star was what is.
A star looks backwards,
says the sea.

BEFORE I GO

first let me thank my sneakers
for raising me an inch, freshwater
for always being there, even
in cubes, I have so many

T-cells I'm afraid of forgetting
their names, really gasoline got me
where I am today, the sky also
made an impact, I truly

can't say enough about space,
so many families of galaxies
gathered around, a few footprints
on the moon & earth but none

between, like an unworn
patch of ice & once I step off
this stage you'll clear me
from your mind, you'll enter

delete in one sense water
takes the shape of anything,
in another it simply rests
its head forever

HOW TO TALK TO THE MOON

raise your voice above   the lights of the city

the street sweeping   the hills the clouds

in no rush   clear your throat

loosen the knots   in your chest

like a hundred strings from a hundred

black balloons   there's nothing

in the sky you can't stab with a pin

there's nowhere   too cool for a flag

everyone is welcome   even your friends

of friends   when the moon is full

the sea cranes   its long neck

the stars floating   on their backs

their lips   gone so blue

NO OTHER WAY

land isn't part of the ocean

therefore it rises
against it

REMAINING ON POINT

To the ground, a tree is tangential. The sky's

always on the fence. Really, I can't decide when,

where, or how. Dear ex, are you still there?

On the other line? All I know is please

remove your heels before flooding my memory.

When you text, my cell flashes one brief

minute of life remaining. In that span

I could bungee from head to toe. I could fit

my favorite loneliness for a gown, sequins sparkling

the light-years away. Dimmer, less naked to

the eye. Like a space bar pushing us farther apart

on the page. Across seven continents & six thousand

spoken languages, the world shares only one word

& that's *Coca-Cola*. I could enter anywhere

in the story, raise my tall glass, & be somebody.

Isn't it something, spinning all day? Isn't the earth

in charge of us never drifting too far?

There's no antenna on my phone.

It's always for you.

THEN

one day the world
snowballs into a far
sweeter memory

not even pigeon hawks
not even a snapped

branch can fly
back where it began

IN ZERO GRAVITY

I'll flip my mind like a silver coin.

I'll weigh less & less with each step, my eyes late

to their sockets. Between this spaceship

    & my piece-of-crap car, there can be

no comparison. Between here & home,

               there are miles of darkness

in my heart. No explorer goes that deep:

      Columbus discovered nothing but his own likeness

etched in city squares, his granite face

fixed on, who really cares—the truth is so much

         less engraved. The truth is

      sailing across the sea & the sadness of

not wrecking. I remember the boats

upon boats. If one fills with water,

                                        it veers away

from what it knows,

starts a new life entirely.

ACKNOWLEDGMENTS

I'm grateful to the editors of the following journals where these poems—or earlier versions—can be found.

Adroit Journal, Agni, The Awl, Barrow Street, Boston Review, Carolina Quarterly, Colorado Review, Columbia: A Journal of Literature & Art, Crab Creek Review, Cream City Review, Denver Quarterly, DIAGRAM, Field, Four Way Review, Hayden's Ferry Review, Kenyon Review, The Literary Review, Narrative, New Orleans Review, The New Yorker, Pleiades, Ploughshares, Poetry Northwest, Prelude Magazine, and *Tin House Online.*

Thanks to London's Design Museum for featuring an excerpt from "Remaining on Point" in their 2015 exhibit on brands.

I'm indebted to so many kind and brilliant people who helped shape this manuscript throughout its development. Firstly, to Jay Deshpande, Lizzie Harris, and Jenny Xie, who read countless revisions and contributed more than I can say here, as well as Andrew Eisenman, Michael Homolka, Jen Levitt, and Amy Meng. I'm grateful also for friends who commented on individual poems—including many that rightly didn't make the cut—or offered encouraging words. Thanks to Kaveh Akbar, Abba Belgrave, Rio Cortez, Adam Dalva, Alex Dimitrov, Hafizah Geter, Kelly Forsythe, Peter Longofono, David McLoghlin, Brandon Menke, Rachel Morgenstern-Clarren, Jennifer Nelson, Morgan Parker, Maya Popa, Cat Richardson, Curtis Rogers, Charif Shanahan, Solmaz Sharif, Jessi Stevens, Lindsay Turner, Jeannie Vanasco, Eric Weinstein, Marina Weiss, and Stephen Weiss.

I'm indebted to my teachers and mentors: David Baker, Breyten Breytenbach, Eduardo C. Corral, Martín Espada, Jorie Graham, Yusef Komunyakaa, Deborah Landau, Betsy LaPadula, Maureen N. McLane, Meghan O'Rourke, Matthew Rohrer, Brenda Shaughnessy, and Erica Wright. I'm thankful also for the supportive communities I've found. Thank you to writers and friends at New York University, Harvard University, Newark Academy, Vermont Studio Center, and Bread Loaf, as well as Interbrand and VSA.

Thanks to the Four Way Books team, especially Bridget Bell, Clarissa Long, James Moore, Ryan Murphy, and Martha Rhodes.

Thanks to Lan Lam for designing the cover, and to Siddhartha Sinha for taking the author photo.

Finally, my love to my family for all they have given me. To Beverly, Dorothy, NSDB. To my parents and their parents. To Victoria.

Publication of this book was made possible by grants and donations. We are also grateful to those individuals who participated in our 2017 Build a Book Program. They are:

Anonymous (6), Evan Archer, Sally Ball, Jan Bender-Zanoni, Zeke Berman, Kristina Bicher, Laurel Blossom, Carol Blum, Betsy Bonner, Mary Brancaccio, Lee Briccetti, Deirdre Brill, Anthony Cappo, Carla & Steven Carlson, Caroline Carlson, Stephanie Chang, Tina Chang, Liza Charlesworth, Maxwell Dana, Machi Davis, Marjorie Deninger, Lukas Fauset, Monica Ferrell, Emily Flitter, Jennifer Franklin, Martha Webster & Robert Fuentes, Chuck Gillett, Dorothy Goldman, Dr. Lauri Grossman, Naomi Guttman & Jonathan Mead, Steven Haas, Mary Heilner, Hermann Hesse, Deming Holleran, Nathaniel Hutner, Janet Jackson, Christopher Kempf, David Lee, Jen Levitt, Howard Levy, Owen Lewis, Paul Lisicky, Sara London & Dean Albarelli, David Long, Katie Longofono, Cynthia Lowen, Ralph & Mary Ann Lowen, Donna Masini, Louise Mathias, Catherine McArthur, Nathan McClain, Gregory McDonald, Britt Melewski, Kamilah Moon, Carolyn Murdoch, Rebecca & Daniel Okrent, Tracey Orick, Zachary Pace, Gregory Pardlo, Allyson Paty, Marcia & Chris Pelletiere, Taylor Pitts, Eileen Pollack, Barbara Preminger, Kevin Prufer, Vinode Ramgopal, Martha Rhodes, Roni & Richard Schotter, Peter & Jill Schireson, Soraya Shalforoosh, Peggy Shinner, James Snyder & Krista Fragos, Megan Staffel, Alice St. Claire-Long, Robin Taylor, Marjorie & Lew Tesser, Boris Thomas, Judith Thurman, Susan Walton, Calvin Wei, Abby Wender, Bill Wenthe, Allison Benis White, Elizabeth Whittlesey, Hao Wu, Monica Youn, and Leah Zander.